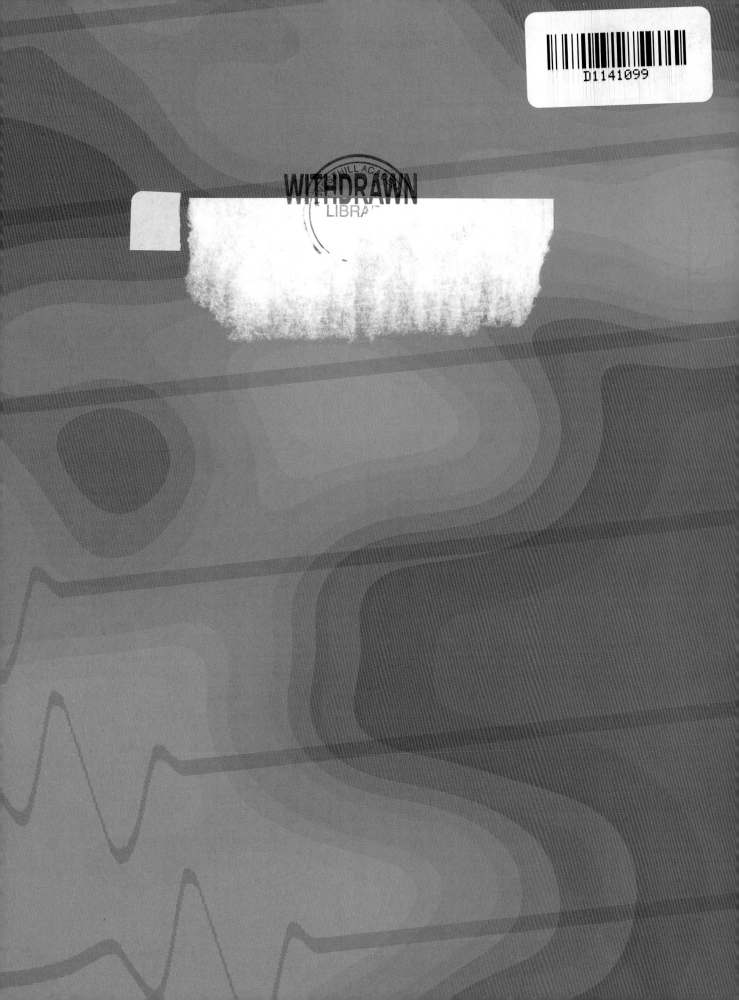

It's Your Health!

Self-esteem

JILLIAN POWELL

FRANKLIN WATTS
LONDON•SYDNEY

First published in 2004 by Franklin Watts
96 Leonard Street, London EC2A 4XD

Franklin Watts Australia
45-51 Huntley Street, Alexandria, NSW 2015

Series editor: Sarah Peutrill
Editor: Sarah Ridley
Designed by: Pewter Design Associates
Series design: Peter Scoulding
Picture researcher: Sophie Hartley
Series consultant: Wendy Anthony, Health Education Unit, Education Service, Birmingham City Council
Picture credits: © Paul Baldesare/Photofusion: 16, 22, 24, 27t, 36t. © Joe Bator/Corbis: 15b. © Bettmann/Corbis: 9t. Photo from www.JohnBirdsall.co.uk: 23b. Brand X Pictures/Alamy: 41. © Robert Brook/Photofusion: 32b. Peter Brooker/Rex Features: 29t. © Graham Burns/Photofusion: 38. © Jacky Chapman/Photofusion: 14, 30b. Crollalanza/Rex Features: 12. Chris Fairclough/Franklin Watts: 4, 11t, 11b, 17b, 17t, 19b, 20, 21, 23t, 37b, 45. FBA/Rex Features: 32t. © Melanie Friend/Photofusion: 31. © Raymond Gehman/Corbis: 39b. Gusto/Science Photo Library: 25b. © Debbie Humphry/Photofusion: 28. Ali Kabas/Alamy: 40. © Reed Kaestner/Corbis: 13b. © Ute Klaphake/Photofusion: 25t. © Clarissa Leahy/Photofusion: 10. © Colin McPherson/Corbis: 35. Ray Moller/Franklin Watts: 36b. Jeff Morgan/Alamy: 33. © Jose Luis Pelaez, Inc./Corbis: 9b. © Michael Pole/Corbis: 34. © Rob & Sas/Corbis: 37t. © Norbert Schaefer/Corbis: 19t. © Paula Solloway/Photofusion: 18. © Tom Stewart/Corbis: 27b. Vinnie Suffante/Rex Features: 30t. Topham Picturepoint: 29b. © David Tothill/Photofusion: 39t. U.S. National Institute of Health/Science Photo Library: 26. © Bob Watkins/Photofusion: 15t. Janine Wiedel Photolibrary/Alamy: 8. World Religions Photo Library/Alamy: 13t. Every attempt has been made to clear copyright. Should there be any inadvertent omission, please apply to the publisher for rectification.

The Publisher would like to thank the Brunswick Club for Young People, Fulham, London for their help with this book. Thanks to our models, including Spencer Thoroughgood and Stevie Waite.

A CIP catalogue record for this book is available from the British Library

ISBN 0 7496 5569 0

Printed in Malaysia

Contents

What is self-esteem?

Self-esteem is how we think and feel about ourselves. It refers to how we think about the way we look, our abilities, our relationships with others and our hopes for the future. We are not born with self-esteem – it is something we develop as we grow older.

All these teenagers look as if they are having a good time but it is difficult to know what is really going on inside other people's heads. We need to develop a positive inner voice and try not to doubt other people's feelings towards us to be happy.

Opinion not fact

Self-esteem is based on our inner feelings, not on facts. Research has shown that there is often a wide gap between how we are seen and how we think we are seen. Self-esteem can be an important factor in our lives. It can affect our health, our career decisions and relationships, and also the way we deal with problems we may have to face, such as bullying, or peer pressure. It is an important factor in making us feel happy.

The American psychologist William James (1842-1910).

It is good to be realistic about our own abilities as we can then feel positive about results, knowing we have tried our hardest.

Social identity

Psychologists have been studying self-esteem since William James first wrote about it over 100 years ago. He wrote about our ideas of self and social identity – how we see ourselves in relation to a wider society or community.

Today, many work places and schools see improving the self-esteem of their employees or pupils as one of their goals. They believe that we can only respect others if we respect ourselves. If we have a sense of our own worth, we are more likely to value others and act responsibly towards them.

Respect!

Having high self-esteem means we feel positive about ourselves as individuals, and in comparison to others. It means we value our strengths and feel in control of our lives and our futures. With high self-esteem, the world feels like a good place full of friends and people who respond positively to us.

How do we get self-esteem?

Self-esteem begins to be formed when we are babies. When we cry, if someone feeds us and cuddles us, we feel that we are loved and valued. We begin to trust our parent or carer, knowing that they keep us safe and well. As we get older, we look to the people around us for approval as well. The feeling that we are valued by them is the basis of our self-esteem.

Even when we are babies, the way our parents behave towards us is important for our self-esteem.

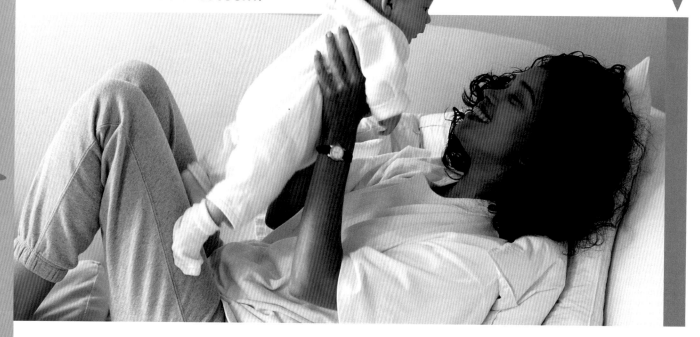

Family matters

Experts agree that our family helps form our vision of ourselves, particularly when we are babies or young children. Parents who talk to their children respectfully, without put-downs, praise their children and show them how loved they are, will help their children develop good feelings about themselves.

Even as we grow up, the way our parents behave towards us affects our self-esteem. We feel better about ourselves if our parents are supportive of our aims and proud of our achievements. It helps if parents or carers give us some control over our lives and choices.

We may inherit our self-esteem, in part, through our genes. Studies of twins have shown that they are often alike in their self-esteem, whether it is high or low, even if they have been separated at birth and brought up by different parents. Scientists are studying this, to understand whether there is a gene that affects our self-esteem.

Comparisons

When we go to school, we meet friends and teachers who also influence the way we feel about ourselves. We may start to compare ourselves with other children who we feel are somehow 'better' than we are - cleverer or better-looking. Our academic abilities are also compared through tests and exams.

It's your opinion

Some studies have shown that girls are likely to have slightly lower self-esteem than boys. The gap is widest when they are in their late teens. Do you think that boys have naturally higher self-esteem than girls? If so, why do you think this is?

▲ Teenage girls often feel under pressure to look good.

People and events

As we become adults, our self-esteem is affected by people we meet and by events in our lives. We are constantly judging ourselves, often in comparison with others. The way we feel about ourselves does not stay the same – it changes as our lives change.

If we have success at school, or work, and meet people who love us and value us, we feel good. If a relationship goes wrong, or if we fail an important exam, we can feel low. Good friends can help us maintain our self-esteem at times like these. But people who don't make us feel good about ourselves are best avoided.

It's your decision

Are you too competitive?
How you feel about yourself can depend on how you compare yourself with others. But this can make us too competitive, which can lead to unhappiness if we feel we fail to measure up. We need to be careful we don't become so competitive that we undermine our self-esteem – or someone else's.

As we become older, the opinions of our friends become as important as those of our family. ▶

Measuring self-esteem

Our self-esteem is based on standards set not just by family and friends, but by the community and culture that we live in. These standards vary within communities, ethnic groups and cultures.

We may look up to glamorous film stars and measure our success next to them – but they too enjoy boosts to their self-esteem through award ceremonies such as the Oscars, shown here.

Celebrity culture

In Western cultures, the lifestyles of pop stars, film stars, models and sportspeople are celebrated. Many people long to be slim, good-looking and wealthy, living in expensive homes, just like these famous people. If we live in a Western culture our self-esteem may be partly based on how we see ourselves in relation to these ideals – whether we 'measure up' or not. We are encouraged to be competitive and to value individual success and wealth.

It's your opinion

Should we base our self-esteem on how we measure up to cultural ideals like good looks and wealth? What do we risk if we do this? What makes a successful person?

Community values

In contrast, many non-Western cultures do not place importance on individual success. They measure self-esteem in terms of how much individuals contribute to the family or community around them. Even physical ideals may be different from Western models; for example, in parts of Africa, being thin is seen as a sign of poverty, so it's desirable to be plump or overweight.

The Sikh culture emphasises involvement with the community. Here, Sikh women volunteer to cook at their local temple.

Gender and age

In some cultures, such as in China, Japan and India, boys are valued more highly than girls because they are seen as bringing wealth and security to a family, while girls cost the family money in marriage settlements.

Our age may also influence the way we feel about ourselves, depending on the values of the culture we live in. Western cultures worship youth, so many older people feel left out and undervalued. But many Asian and African cultures respect and value the wisdom and understanding that comes with old age. Older people in these societies are more likely to feel valued.

Grandparents in Japan play an active part in family life, and are valued for the experience age brings.

It's your experience

'My brother is really good at sport, sports captain in his year and all that. I've never been good at sport, and I can't help feeling I am letting the side down – Dad was a good sportsman too.'

Giles, aged 15

13

High self-esteem

Self-esteem is an important part of our health and wellbeing. If we feel good about ourselves, we are more likely to look after our health by making sensible choices, such as eating a balanced diet and avoiding smoking and drugs. We will have the confidence to make decisions that are right for us. It also helps us to get through difficult or stressful times and events in our lives.

Knowing our own mind

Self-esteem is all about valuing ourselves. It means we are less likely to go along with our friends if they are doing something stupid or dangerous – like joy-riding or taking drugs. By knowing our own mind, we can be smart enough to make our own decisions, even if others are trying to persuade us otherwise.

Dealing with problems

We all have problems to deal with at some time in our lives. All these events can affect us, and make us doubt ourselves. But if we have a healthy sense of inner-self, we can bounce back and be less affected by criticism or rejection. We know our own strengths, whatever others say or do.

▼ If we are lucky enough to have good friends, this can give us high self-esteem.

Sophie's 18th birthday

▲ When we reach the age of consent we have to take more responsibility for ourselves. Having high self-esteem gives us more confidence in our decisions.

Making choices

High self-esteem gives us the confidence to try new things and learn from our mistakes. It means we are open to advice and criticism, but we also have the self-belief to make our own choices, without needing the approval of others.

People with high self-esteem are able to risk failure because they know they will be able to cope with it and even try again. But this does not mean having such a high opinion of ourselves that we can't accept criticism, or feel we never make any mistakes. If we feel like that, we are less likely to learn and grow with our experiences.

It's your experience

'My family set their hearts on me becoming a doctor, but I have known right from the start that it wasn't right for me. I want to be an actress – I know it's going to be really hard, but I have to try.'

Aleema, aged 19

▲ Our ability to get over and learn from our failures, such as failing a driving test, is determined by our self-esteem.

It's your decision

Are you prepared to take risks?
Can you laugh at yourself and not take yourself too seriously? If you are terrified of failure or of looking foolish, you may protect yourself from challenges that could help you grow.

Growing up

How we feel about ourselves changes at different times in our lives. When we are growing up, our bodies start to change as we go through puberty. These changes can make us very aware of our body image. Puberty affects the way we feel, too. The hormones rushing round in our blood can make us feel moody and emotional. It's an unsettling time.

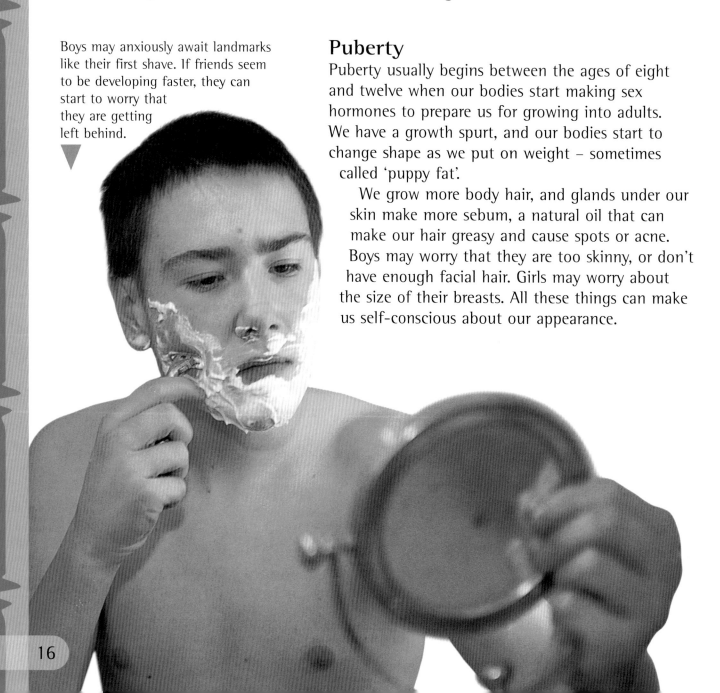

Boys may anxiously await landmarks like their first shave. If friends seem to be developing faster, they can start to worry that they are getting left behind.

Puberty

Puberty usually begins between the ages of eight and twelve when our bodies start making sex hormones to prepare us for growing into adults. We have a growth spurt, and our bodies start to change shape as we put on weight – sometimes called 'puppy fat'.

We grow more body hair, and glands under our skin make more sebum, a natural oil that can make our hair greasy and cause spots or acne. Boys may worry that they are too skinny, or don't have enough facial hair. Girls may worry about the size of their breasts. All these things can make us self-conscious about our appearance.

It's your decision

Can you make the best of yourself?
There are some things we can't change about ourselves, like how tall we grow. But we can make sure we learn basic grooming – keeping ourselves fresh with daily showers or baths, and looking after ourselves to make the best of the way we look.

Teenagers can be very self-critical. Many would like to change the way they look.

Sexuality

As sex hormones start pumping round our body, we become aware of our sexuality. We start to feel sexual attraction towards others, and may have fantasies about sexual partners, such as pop or sports idols, or people we know. If we approach someone we fancy and they show no interest in us or reject us, it is a blow. Media images constantly tell us we should be sexy and desirable, so if we feel we fail to measure up, we can feel a failure.

Feeling different

If we find we are attracted to the same sex, we may feel that family or friends are expecting us to be heterosexual, and that they will be disappointed. We may try to hide our sexuality. Coming to terms with our sexuality and being able to express it in our relationships is part of our wellbeing.

Problem skin is common in teenage years. It can knock confidence badly.

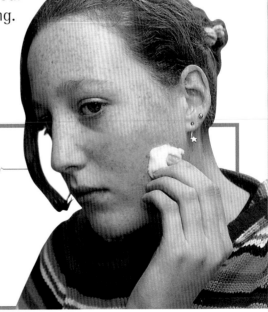

It's your experience

'My skin never really feels clean now. Having zits is a real downer when you're on a date. You feel like everyone is looking at them.'

Rachel, aged 15

Life events

Our self-esteem can be influenced by events in our lives. Important changes, like family or relationship break-up, or coping with the death of someone close, challenge our emotions. We can't control many of these events, but they can still affect the way we see ourselves. Making new friends or achieving success in something can make us feel good about ourselves again.

Exam results can be good or bad – can you cope with either? ▼

You win some, you lose some

As we grow up, we all need to accept the successes and failures in our own lives. If your team loses a match, it is good to talk over the disappointment – getting angry won't help.

If you feel disappointed with a school result, talk it over with your parents, or a friend or teacher. You can always do better next time. Learn to develop a range of emotional reactions to events and keep talking to people you trust.

These relatively small events can also be useful, however, because they can help us deal with bigger crises when these arise.

It's your experience

'When my boyfriend told me he was seeing someone else, I felt like I'd been kicked in the stomach. It had been going on for ages, and I found out later that everyone seemed to know about it except me. I felt really stupid, and I also felt hurt.'

Mel, aged 19

Rejection

Whenever we feel rejected or hurt by others, it knocks us back. Children who go into care often have low self-esteem because they feel rejected, even though their parents may love them but cannot look after them.

Adults have to deal with some tough situations too: from a partner leaving or being unfaithful, to losing a job or dealing with health worries. Talking through these events and learning to forgive can help.

Family break-up

When parents break up, it can be very unsettling for everyone involved. Children may have to move home or school, and see less of one parent. They may feel that they themselves have done something wrong. If a parent leaves home and no longer stays in touch, the child may feel that they have lost that parent's love. They may begin to have problems at school, and often their schoolwork suffers. Research shows that five years after a family break-up, over a third of all children still feel depressed.

Bereavement

When someone close to us dies, life is very tough because we have lost someone who made us feel good by loving and caring for us. The loss of their love leaves a gap in our lives. We may even feel guilty that we did not tell them how much we loved them, or we may feel upset about the way we behaved to them before they died.

The break-up of a family is stressful and upsetting for all involved. Children may often appear to be coping, but they will be dealing with difficult feelings and their home and school lives may suffer.

Losing a loved one is difficult at any age. ▶

It's your opinion

Young adults from broken families are nearly twice as likely as others to need special help, such as counselling. Why do you think this is? What do you think will help these children rebuild their inner happiness?

The effects of low self-esteem

Low self-esteem can affect every area of our lives, from our relationships and work to our health and wellbeing. It can mean we don't take proper care of ourselves, because inside we don't feel we are worth taking care of. If we don't respect and value ourselves, we are unlikely to respect and value others, so it can affect the way we behave towards others, too.

Self-criticism

From our earliest years, we look for approval and encouragement from those around us. So if our parents criticise us, or our friends make fun of us, our self-esteem can be harmed. If we are constantly told that we are unattractive, or stupid or worthless, we will in time begin to feel all those things inside. We learn to criticise ourselves, and blame ourselves when things go wrong.

It is natural for everyone to feel down at times - but if the feelings don't lift, we may need to seek help.

Feeling low

Feeling low will obviously make people feel unhappy and can even lead to an illness called depression (see pages 26-27). We may be afraid of trying new things, because we are scared we will fail. We may compare ourselves with others, who we feel are smarter and more attractive than we are. Even people who appear to us to have everything – looks, brains and money – may feel low inside because they see themselves differently from the way others see them.

It's your decision

Do you help around the house? Parents often nag their children to tidy bedrooms or help with the washing up. You could be doing yourself a big favour by learning how to keep your room tidy and how to shop for food and prepare meals. It is a huge boost to self-confidence to know that you can live independently.

Taking risks

If we have low self-esteem, we may put our health at risk. People with low self-esteem are more likely to become addicted to tobacco, drugs or alcohol.

We may also take risks with our sexual health by having sex before we feel ready, or by failing to practise safe sex, and not using a condom. People may stay in violent and unhappy relationships because they feel the problems are their fault, or they don't feel they deserve better.

Low expectations

Research shows that low self-esteem increases the risk of teenage pregnancy. Some girls may see pregnancy as their only means of getting social status and living independently. These girls may not see that there are other choices, such as getting more qualifications that could lead to a rewarding job and a better lifestyle.

Surveys also show a link between low self-esteem and unemployment for young men. If they feel they are unable to compete in the job market, unemployment may seem to be a safe option.

▲ Work gives us purpose and interest - but it can all feel like too much of an effort if our job prospects seem poor.

Improve your self-esteem

Select ten words from the box that reflect your own qualities and display a list of them in a prominent place:

adventurous	free	patient
ambitious	funny	polite
alert	generous	pleasant
affectionate	gentle	persistent
artistic	growing	practical
brave	happy	punctual
calm	healthy	quiet
caring	helpful	relaxed
capable	honest	reliable
cheerful	hopeful	responsible
clever	imaginative	special
confident	inventive	sporty
determined	kind	strong
dependable	loving	tactful
easy-going	likeable	thorough
energetic	modest	trusting
faithful	open-minded	warm
fit	out-going	witty

It's your opinion

The UK and the US have some of the highest rates for teenage pregnancy in the world. What do you think are the main causes, and what could be done to reduce the numbers?

Body image

Our body image – the way we see and think about our body – is an important part of self-esteem. We may see ourselves as fat or skinny, worry that our nose is too big, or think our ears stick out too much. We may compare our body with others', and be influenced by what others say about us. If we get teased or bullied because of the way we look, this can make us feel worse.

Media images

Experts believe that our body image is influenced by media images that tell us we have to look young and slim to be beautiful, desirable or successful. This can lead to poor body image, as we compare ourselves negatively with the ideals we see.

In the UK, one survey showed that almost 80 per cent of women think about their body shape every day, and only 1 per cent of women are completely happy with their body. Other studies have shown that many girls have a poor body image by the age of 13.

Dolls like these impress Western ideals of youth and beauty on little girls.

Boys may also feel dissatisfied with the way they look – perhaps they feel they are too short, or have a poor physique. Some may feel they have to exercise or take drugs such as steroids, to try and improve their body.

We get many of our ideas on image from magazines and the media.

It's your experience

'I have a skin complaint that makes my skin look red and scaly. I don't want to go swimming with my mates any more – I feel like everyone is thinking "Gross!"'

Patsy, aged 16

It's your decision

Would you support a bully?
People may be teased or called names because of the way they look but we should always remember that teasing or bullying someone because of their appearance will hurt their feelings and lower their self-esteem.

Healthy body image

Most of us have something we would like to change about our body, but we all have some good features. Having a healthy body image means accepting the things we can't change about ourselves, and learning how to make the most of our best features.

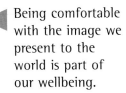

Being comfortable with the image we present to the world is part of our wellbeing.

Problems and changes

Unfortunately, accidents or illness can change our appearance. If we are left with a disability or scarring we can become self-conscious about the way we look to others. We may need help from counsellors or psychiatrists to achieve a feeling of acceptance about how we now look.

Eating disorders

Low self-esteem, based on poor body image, has been linked with eating disorders including anorexia nervosa and bulimia nervosa. Anyone can develop an eating disorder, although young women are most at risk.

Widespread problem

In the UK, around 165,000 people are affected – one in ten of them are males. Some estimates suggest up to a million men and boys, and 10 million women and girls in the US suffer some form of eating disorder. There have been some cases of anorexia nervosa in children as young as three.

Different types

There are several types of eating disorder. Someone who has anorexia nervosa will starve themselves of food and drink, often skipping meals and pretending to others that they have eaten. When someone has bulimia nervosa they will binge-eat, often in secret, then make themselves sick to get rid of the food so they don't gain weight.

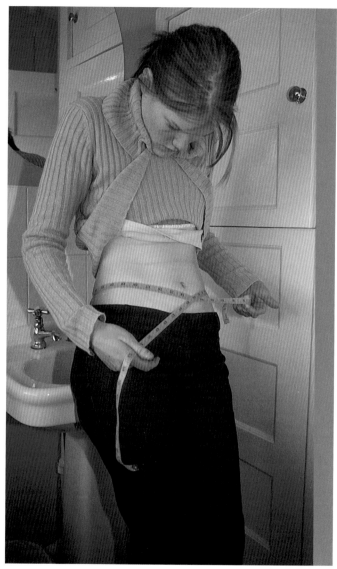

An eating disorder such as anorexia makes sufferers obsessive about their size and weight.

It's your experience

'When you have an eating disorder you don't see yourself as others see you. You can be skin and bones and you still think you look fat.'

Belinda, aged 15 (recovering anorexic)

Anorexics and bulimics see themselves as fat even when they are dangerously thin, or even close to death.

Binge-eating – eating much more food than the body needs, often in secret and without feeling hungry – is itself an eating disorder. It can harm your body and lead to obesity.

Bulimia often results in feelings of guilt and self-disgust.

Emotional problems and causes

Eating disorders are a way of trying to cope with emotional problems or other difficulties. Sometimes, they can be triggered by stressful events such as bereavement, bullying or abuse. The eating disorder is a way of trying to block out painful feelings or gain total control over body weight, when everything else in life seems out of control.

Some experts believe that eating disorders may be caused by a gene, or by a parent or carer's attitude to food. Others have blamed the rise in cases of eating disorders on the images of super-thin models promoted by the fashion and advertising industries.

Binge-eaters often choose fatty foods like chips and ice-cream for 'comfort eating'.

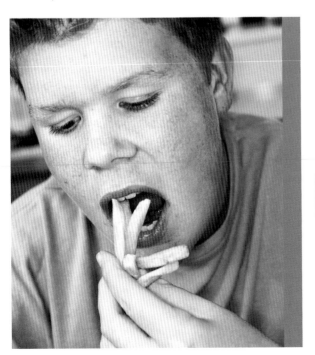

Physical treatment

Eating disorders can lead to great unhappiness and sometimes premature death. In cases of dangerous weight loss or weight gain, a patient will often be treated in hospital. A range of treatments are used to treat the physical body including drugs and surgery. There are continual advances in our understanding and treatment of eating disorders.

Treating underlying problems

Treatment for all eating disorders involves trying to identify and deal with the individual's underlying problem. Is food, or lack of it, filling an emotional gap in the person's life or has something traumatic happened to them? Health professionals can help the patient understand why he or she feels this way and reach a more realistic view of their appearance.

It's your opinion

Experts have criticised the fashion industry for promoting images of underweight models. Do you think these images can encourage dieting and even lead to eating disorders?

Depression

Low self-esteem can sometimes be part of an illness called depression. We all feel low at times, but when these feelings stay with us for a long time and nothing lifts our mood, we may be suffering from depression. Depression affects about one in twenty of us at some time in our lives. Often 'high achievers' who set themselves high standards and goals suffer from this illness.

Brain scans show changes in chemical activity in the brain when someone is depressed.

Symptoms

When someone is feeling depressed, they may feel sad and tearful much of the time. They feel low about themselves and their lives, and they cannot see any way of making things better. They may lose interest in their friends, their hobbies and even in food. They may also sleep a lot, or sleep badly, feel very tired and have no energy.

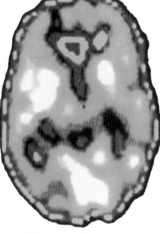

Normal　　　　Depressed

It's your decision

What do you want from your life? Studies show that when children believe money, fame and beauty can bring happiness, they are more likely to suffer from depression. It's worth remembering that even people who seem to 'have it all' can suffer from depression. Research has shown that once the basic costs of living are covered, there is no strong link between the level of happiness and the amount of money an individual owns.

Causes

Scientists think that the way we feel is the result of changes to chemicals in our brain called neurotransmitters. These chemicals affect our mood by stimulating our brain cells. As depression can run in families, scientists think there may be a gene that can influence these brain chemicals and make us more likely to become depressed.

Depression can be triggered by events or changes in our lives, such as the death of someone close to us. It is normal to feel devastated by such events and depression triggered in this way usually heals itself over a period of a few months.

Anti-depressant drugs may help someone through a difficult time.

It's your experience

'I didn't realise how unsettled I was going to feel when we moved house to be nearer to Dad's new job. I'd left my life behind and I felt really low and bad-tempered with everyone for several months. Now I am taking up some of the things I enjoy doing again, so I've started swimming for a club and I'm getting to know a few people.'

Sam, aged 14

Treatment

When depression is lasting, it becomes an illness that needs treatment. Doctors may prescribe drugs called anti-depressants. These work by increasing the levels of important neurotransmitters, such as serotonin, in the brain. Because they are often addictive, doctors limit the period of time that a person takes these drugs. The underlying causes of depression need to be treated, often with some form of therapy.

Talking over problems with a counsellor can give us an insight into why we feel the way we do.

It's your decision

What can you do to make yourself feel good? Many young people feel like they are on a rollercoaster with their emotions. Some experts think that it helps to take walks through woods, or by the sea, as it restores a sense of wonder in the world. It helps to remember what does make you feel good, whether that is rollerblading or drawing, and do much more of it.

Children and depression

People often think of depression as an illness that only affects adults, but children as young as seven years old have been given anti-depressants and there are reports that 20 per cent of children in the UK suffer from emotional problems or depression, often triggered by family break-down.

Self-harm

Sometimes, low self-esteem and depression can lead to self-harm – deliberately harming or injuring our own body. It can mean cutting or burning the skin, pulling out hair, or poisoning the body with harmful drugs. Self-harm is always a sign of unhappiness and low self-esteem.

Physical scars, such as cuts to the arms, are an outward display of inward unhappiness.

Hurting yourself

Some people cut or burn themselves as a way of dealing with difficult feelings. People who self-harm may be feeling trapped and helpless about a problem they cannot solve. It is a way of feeling in control.

The physical pain of the cut distracts from the inner mental pain. In some instances, they may be coping with painful feelings about something that has happened to them, or punishing themselves because they feel guilty or ashamed about something.

A teenager who self-harms may be trying to cope with problems of bullying and abuse or coming to terms with their sexuality. They may be under pressure at school or at home, or having problems with family or friends.

Getting help

People who self-harm often do it secretly, and feel too embarrassed and ashamed to tell others about their problem. If they are cutting or burning their skin, they may cover up the scars with long sleeves to keep their secret hidden. They need to get help because they are putting their health at risk. Scars from self-harm may be lasting, and can lead to blood-poisoning and infections.

A recent survey carried out by the Samaritans discovered that 50 per cent of the young people they interviewed had tried to seek help before they hurt themselves. Some people will need specialist help from a doctor or youth counsellor.

Substance abuse

Abusing drugs and other harmful substances can be another symptom of deliberate self-harm. Smoking, drinking too much alcohol, and taking drugs can all harm our health. Smoking damages our lungs and can cause heart disease and cancer.

Drinking heavily, especially binge-drinking, can lead to problems including heart and liver disease. Drugs can damage our physical and mental health.

All these substance are addictive, so our mind and body can come to depend on them and need them. If we value and respect ourselves, we will avoid taking these risks to our health and wellbeing.

▲ Alcoholism can lead to loss of our health, job and home.

Even 'soft' drug-use, such as smoking cannabis, ▶ can be a sign that someone is trying to escape their problems. If these problems are not solved, they may go on to try other drugs.

It's your opinion

Surveys show that self-harm affects more teenage girls than boys – and that it is also more likely in young children living in one-parent families. Why do you think these groups are most at risk?

Bullying and abuse

Bullying, abuse and peer pressure can make us feel desperate about our lives. It can be hard to stand our ground when someone is bullying or abusing us, or when our peers are trying to persuade us to do something we don't want to do. Bullying happens to almost all of us at some point in our lives. We owe it to ourselves to try to sort out the situation so that the bullying stops.

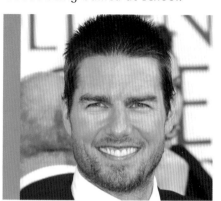

The American actor Tom Cruise has spoken openly about being bullied at school.

Bullying

Bullying can be verbal – such as calling someone names, insulting or threatening them. It can also be physical, such as hitting or pushing someone around. Someone who is being bullied can feel unhappy and afraid. They may feel ashamed that they are not able to stand up to the bully.

Bullies themselves may appear confident, but this can be a front. Bullying may be their only way of getting status within their peer group. Sometimes they are being bullied themselves, and take their feelings out on others.

Bullying can start from a young age and can make life a misery for the victim.

It's your opinion

It is very easy for adults or older brothers or sisters to correct, criticise or even bully the younger members of the family. Often people hardly realise they are doing it, yet it can take away the confidence of the young person. Do you behave in this way? Can you think of other ways to communicate?

NO ONE DESERVES TO BE BULLIED

If you are being bullied at school, follow your school's anti-bullying policy, whether it is to tell the nominated teacher or put a note in the bully box. If your school doesn't have a policy, try some of the following:

- Tell a friend - it is harder for a bully to stand up to two people.
- Try to ignore the comments. The bully is looking for a reaction - if you don't give one, the bully may get bored.
- Don't fight back - most bullies are bigger than the person they are picking on and also you could end up being blamed for the situation and make it all a lot worse.
- Try to think up clever responses in advance, or try to make a joke of it all.
- Keep a record so that an adult can see how often you are being bullied.

Abuse

When one person abuses another, they do or say things to them that make them feel unhappy and uncomfortable. Sexual abuse means touching someone in a sexual way, when they do not want to be touched. Sexual abuse can make someone feel ashamed that the abuse is somehow their fault, but this is never the case.

Domestic violence is another form of abuse. It means violence that takes place in a home when one person hits, punches or physically hurts another. The abuser could be a parent or a brother or sister. Any form of abuse is wrong and has to be stopped.

Some women need to find a safe house or refuge to escape abuse by partners. ▶

Peer pressure

Sometimes our friends, or peers, may try to persuade us to do something we don't really want to do. This is called 'peer pressure'. If our self-esteem is low, we may give in to peer pressure to try and win approval and feel that we belong. We are not confident enough in our own ideas and views, so we go along with the crowd.

High self-esteem helps us resist peer pressure. We have enough self-confidence to make our own decisions, and stick to them even if we risk making others dislike us or make fun of us.

It's your experience

'I got in with a crowd who were always skipping classes and bunking off school. I didn't really want to because I was getting really behind with schoolwork, but they gave me such grief if I said no, it was just easier to go along with it.'

Todd, aged 16

31

Community life

Self-esteem affects society as well as individuals. A nation's self-esteem can be boosted by a big sports win. The self-esteem of a town or city, a street or a block of flats, can be boosted by community events or awards – or damaged by social problems including vandalism, graffiti, gun and gang crime.

When Brazil won the football World Cup in 2002, the nation came together to party.

Anti-social behaviour

Some experts blame low self-esteem for rising rates of crime such as graffiti, burglaries and vandalism, and other anti-social behaviour such as littering and noise pollution. They argue that if individuals don't have respect for themselves, they won't respect others or their property, either. In the US, some communities have developed social policies to improve self-esteem, because they believe it can act as a 'social vaccine', protecting society against anti-social and destructive behaviour.

Litter is a sign that we don't care about our environment, or the people that live in it.

Truancy

Children with low self-esteem are more likely to truant from school. They may be facing problems at home, with their schoolwork or with bullying. Truanting can also be a way of trying to win status and approval from their peers. In the UK, an estimated 7.5 million school days are missed each year through truancy. This can lead to poor education and qualifications, and also increase the risk of crime and anti-social behaviour by these young people while out of school.

These young people are learning DJ skills on a youth project.

Community events

Some people are fortunate enough to live in areas where there is a lot going on. Young people can join youth groups, drama clubs, music and dance groups, sports teams, guides or scouts – mostly run by adults who give their free time to be involved in the community.

Some governments are realising that communities can be helped to function much better if they are given access to these kinds of opportunity. Projects where people are given access to sports facilities, or community theatre or arts projects, can create links across different age groups.

Get involved if you see or hear about projects like this in your area – you'll make new friends and it can boost your self-confidence, especially if you discover you have hidden talents.

It's your opinion

While some experts believe low self-esteem causes many social problems, others argue that there is no evidence for a link – and that people who show anti-social behaviour are more likely to have such high self-esteem that they feel fearless and take risks. Which do you think is true?

It's your decision

Do you respect your community?
We can all help improve our community in the way we treat our neighbours and in how we look after our environment. By putting litter in the bin, by being kind to new neighbours, and thinking of others when enjoying ourselves (for example, by keeping the noise down), we will make people feel more positive about us and our community.

Boosting self-esteem

Studies show that low self-esteem is linked to poor health and wellbeing, and to social problems. This has led to the introduction of courses, programmes and social policies designed to improve self-esteem. A self-esteem industry has grown up, offering everything from guided courses, counselling and group therapy, to self-help books and CDs.

Adventure training courses teach physical skills, but this in turn boosts feelings of confidence and self-worth.

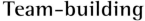

Team-building

Courses designed to improve self-esteem often include team-building exercises, where people learn to work together to achieve a shared goal. Exercises such as one person leading another, blindfolded, over an obstacle such as a river, are designed to build a feeling of trust, which is an important part of our relationship with others. Some may find they have leadership skills, and can encourage others to pull together as part of a team. Others learn that they are a team player, working well alongside others. This knowledge about ourselves can be carried back to school or work, to help us perform our best.

New challenges

Outward-bound or adventure camps and courses are also used to build self-esteem. These courses often include physical challenges, such as exercise circuits or survival exercises in testing places such as mountains or forests. The idea is to set new challenges that stretch our skills and stamina. By achieving difficult goals, we find ourselves capable of more than we expected.

Counselling and courses

Some courses for individuals or groups offer advice and exercises to encourage positive thinking. These can include practical exercises, such as making a pinboard which reminds us of happy experiences, compliments or feedback that we have had. They may suggest thoughts or statements to repeat every day, to train our minds to have positive thoughts about ourselves. Drama and role-play may be used to help us express how we feel about ourselves and our lives.

▲ Special courses, like this boxing class, aim to boost the self-esteem of children who have been bullied.

It's your experience

'Last summer, we went on this outward - bound course. I was terrified at first – I've never been very sporty and I thought I was going to be an embarrassment. But the leaders were great and they encouraged us to have a go at everything. I felt really good about myself when I had done it.'

Jamie, aged 17

Schools

Schools play a huge part in most children's lives. Many schools are following programmes to increase the sense of wellbeing in the children at school. Some schools take the whole-class approach and do exercises especially designed to improve a child's self-image by encouraging children to see all the positive things about themselves. Other teachers pick up on something that a student is really good at, whether it be a talent for art, music, sports or maths, and suggest ways that they could get involved in activities of that nature.

It's your opinion

Do you think activity-style self-esteem courses are good for everyone? Could they ever make matters worse for some people?

Success-a-day

Think about the successes you have experienced through the day, and try to share them with someone. You might find this difficult at first, and then realise that you have learnt something or done something that amounts to a success.

Health and wellbeing

Self-esteem is part of our general health and wellbeing. If we value ourselves, we are more likely to look after our health and make sensible choices for ourselves. This includes thinking about what we eat and getting plenty of exercise and sleep, as well as avoiding health risks.

▲ Personal grooming is the outward sign that we care for ourselves.

Diet

In countries such as France and Italy, many families still sit down to enjoy meals together. They share stories about the day and discuss what is going on in each other's lives. In other countries, more people now 'graze' – eating fast foods at different times of the day. Often these fast foods, or 'junk foods', are high in fat, sugar or salt, and low in healthy nutrients and vitamins.

To avoid the short bursts of energy that sweet or fatty foods give our bodies, you need to eat a balanced diet, with plenty of fresh fruit and vegetables. These foods provide us with the vitamins and minerals we need to stay healthy, and improve our wellbeing and energy levels. Eating them will give our bodies the strength to keep well and allow us to do what we want at day or at night.

Many people enjoy eating chocolate because it is high in fat and sugar and can give the body a 'feel-good' kick. But then, 40 minutes later, we may start to crave the next kick. Try to eat healthier snacks, like fruits or a handful of nuts, which don't have this effect. ▼

It's your decision

Many people once thought that getting a suntan, and even smoking, were good for health. Today, we know that they can both cause ageing and cancer – so it is up to us to make the right choices for our health.

Martial arts classes teach physical and mental discipline and skills.

Exercise and keeping clean

Regular exercise is important for keeping our heart and lungs in order, and helps us burn off calories and stay the correct weight. There is also evidence that it reduces stress and depression and lifts our mood. This is because, when we exercise, the pituitary gland releases chemicals called endorphins that make us feel good. Try to take 10-15 minutes of moderate exercise (like brisk walking) every day, and make time for 20 minutes of more vigorous exercise at least three times a week.

Making the best of yourself by washing every day, and after exercise, and keeping your teeth and hair clean, is also important.

It's your opinion

One study in the US found that teenagers who don't exercise are five times more likely to take up drugs, alcohol and crime. Why do you think this is?

Sleep

Adults who work at night are much more likely to suffer from depression. Our bodies need sleep to function properly. It can be difficult in the teenage years because our internal body clock is moving into adult mode, which means that we may not feel tired until 11pm. However, if we still have to rise at 6.30am to catch the school bus, we won't be getting enough sleep.

We should try to get into the habit of being kind to our bodies by relaxing with music or reading after 9pm so that we are more likely to fall asleep earlier.

Sports like pool are a good way of relaxing with friends and learning new skills.

Have fun

By taking up a new sport or learning how to dance or play music in a band, we can set ourselves goals that we can achieve, and this improves our self-esteem. We should all spend some time doing things that we enjoy, and do more of them.

Turning your life around

Everybody feels unsure about themselves – how they look, how many friends they have got, how clever they are – at some time in their lives. For some it is relatively easy to change the way they feel – parents or friends will encourage a new activity or help in another way. Others struggle – whether because their self-esteem has become really low, or because their personal circumstances are difficult. Here are the stories of a few people who found different ways to turn their lives around:

Coming off drugs

'I started using cannabis at the age of 12. By the time I was 13, I was using crack and at 16 I started smoking heroin. My school work started to suffer badly and eventually my sister-in-law found some heroin under my bed and told my mother. Eventually I checked into a drug treatment centre. I like my life now better than it was. I like to be clean. I've got no worries ... I'm not looking for my next load. Today I must admit that I'm happy that I'm finding me. My addiction is not the only thing about me.'

Sanita, aged 16

Getting active

'I've always been labelled "the shy one" in my family and I was happy with that. But now I see other people having a really interesting time at weekends and in the holidays. Also my older sisters have left home and it is really quiet with my parents. I really like being outside, so I've started going to a nature reserve at weekends to help clear pathways. Because we are busy, I don't feel like I have to be talking to people all the time but when we go in for a drink, we've all got something to talk about.

I really look forward to the volunteer weekends – now I do something interesting at the weekend too.'

Stella, aged 15

Sporting differences

'My school is well-known for football, and I'm not much good at it. I always get picked last in our gym class and the teachers seem to like the football players better. Sometimes I'd pretend to be sick on gym-class days, and I used to sit at home and wonder why I was so useless. Then my mum heard about a local basketball group and I went along one day. It took a lot of courage to go because I thought I'd be rubbish at that too. The people there are really nice and I really enjoy the coaching. I've been going for six months now and I've just made the official club

team! I think I am good at sport after all – I just didn't realise, because football just isn't for me.'

Peter, aged 15

Knowing your own mind

'I never really enjoyed going to school and was really worried about what to do when I leave. My parents both went to university and have always been disappointed with my school marks. I used to study more and more to please them, but I never enjoyed it.

Near the end of last year, I did some work experience at a tree nursery. I really enjoyed being outdoors all day and working with my hands. I learned a lot in just one week. Now I know that when I finish school I'm going to work outdoors,

maybe at a tree nursery. My parents won't like it when I tell them, but I know this is what I want.'

Sam, aged 16

Positive thinking

We all talk to ourselves inside our heads, giving ourselves feedback about how we look and how well or badly we have done. If we are constantly putting ourselves down we will feel bad about ourselves. By focusing on our successes, and complimenting ourselves when we have achieved something, we will increase our feelings of self-worth and confidence.

Build self-confidence

Build on your past successes. No matter how bad things may seem, you must admit that you have succeeded at times. These are the thoughts to dwell on – and get your brain to focus on – for future growth and development.

Have fun

Before you go to bed, try listing three things you have enjoyed in the day that made you feel good – and plan to do more tomorrow!

Banish that nasty voice

Write down the nasty things that the voice in your head says and then think of better, more encouraging things to say instead. 'I didn't do very well in that exam – but I did try my best and I think I can do better next time.'

Call yourself stupid?

Do you call yourself stupid if you make a mistake? Do you call yourself a failure if you give up on a diet? If your mistakes are pointed out to you, do you feel as if you are under attack and become defensive? You're only human so treat yourself kindly. Allow yourself to make mistakes and laugh about them.

Replace criticism with encouragement

Encourage yourself and your friends rather than criticising them. Give compliments or a pat on the back. Think about things positively and achieve what you want.

Accept compliments

Do you interpret events and comments in a negative way? If your friend says that your hair looks nice, do you think, 'What was wrong with it yesterday?' Just accept the compliment and think the best of people's comments.

Ask for help

Never be afraid to tell people how you are feeling. Talk to your friends and family or call one of the organisations listed on page 43, such as the Samaritans.

Glossary

Abuse   hurting someone by words or actions which make them feel unhappy or distressed

Addictive   something which the mind and body come to need and depend on

Alcohol abuse   when someone drinks so much alcohol that they are harming their health

Anorexia nervosa   an eating disorder which makes someone starve themselves of food and drink to try and lose weight

Anti-depressants   drugs used to prevent or treat depression

Binge drinking   drinking a lot of alcohol in one session – more than six units of alcohol for a woman and eight for a man

Binge eating   when someone eats more food than their body needs, often in secret, and even when they are not hungry

Body image   how we see our own bodies

Bulimia nervosa   an eating disorder in which someone binge-eats then gets rid of the food by making themselves sick or using drugs that make them go to the toilet

Bullying   using words or actions to make someone feel afraid or to make them do something they don't want to do

Depression   when someone feels low and unhappy and the feelings don't go away

Domestic violence   violence in the home – when one person physically hurts another

Drug abuse   using illegal drugs such as cannabis, heroin or cocaine for recreational purposes

Gene   part of the make up of our bodies and minds that we inherit from our parents

Hormone   a chemical made in our bodies that goes round in our bloodstream

Neurotransmitter   a chemical in the brain that stimulates the brain cells

Nutrient   part of food that we need to keep our bodies healthy

Obesity   being seriously over-weight: with a body mass index of over 30 (body mass index = weight in kilograms ÷ height in m^2)

Peer pressure   when friends the same age as us try to make us do something or behave in a certain way

Pituitary gland   a gland that releases chemicals that control how our body grows and matures

Psychiatrist   a medical expert who studies mental and emotional problems

Psychologist   a medical expert who studies our minds and behaviour

Puberty   the time when our body changes to make us capable of having babies

Self-harm   deliberately harming or injuring our bodies

Vitamins and minerals   important nutrients in food which we need to stay healthy

Further information

Useful websites

www.lifebytes.gov.uk
Facts on health issues including drugs, mental health and smoking.

www.likeitis.org.uk
This website is part of Marie Stopes International. It gives young people access to information about all aspects of sex education and teenage life.

www.readthesigns.org
Lots of information including helplines and organizations which specialize in problems including depression and eating disorders.

www.kidshealth.org
Provides an internet directory of useful articles covering health, puberty and other issues.

UK charities
Kidscape
A charity committed to keeping children safe from abuse, including bullying and sexual abuse.

2 Grosvenor Gardens
London, SW1W 0DH
Phone: 020 7730 3300
Fax: 020 7730 7081
Helpline: 08451 205 204
www.kidscape.org.uk

Samaritans
Samaritans offers 24-hour confidential support online or by phone for emotional problems.

The Upper Mill, Kingston Road
Ewell, Surrey, KT17 2AF
Tel: 020 8394 8300
Fax: 020 8394 8301
www.samaritans.org.uk

Mind
National charity dedicated to mental health with helplines, drop-in centres, counselling etc.

15-19 Broadway,
London E15 4BQ
Tel: 020 8519 2122
www.mind.org.uk

Australian websites and charities
Kidshelp
Runs a telephone helpline for children in need.

Helpline: 1800 55 1800
www.kidshelp.com.au

www.abc.net.au/talkitup
A website about health, strength, happiness and growing into adulthood. It is designed to connect young people across Australia.

Note to parents and teachers: Every effort has been made by the Publishers to ensure that these websites are suitable for children, that they are of the highest educational value, and that they contain no inappropriate or offensive material. However, because of the nature of the Internet, it is impossible to guarantee that the contents of these sites will not be altered. We strongly advise that Internet access is supervised by a responsible adult.

Index